# GAME OF
# SCONES

# GAME OF
# SCONES

## ALL MEN MUST DINE

JAMMY LANNISTER

This edition first published in Great Britain in 2015 by
Orion
an imprint of the Orion Publishing Group Ltd
Carmelite House
50 Victoria Embankment
London EC4Y 0DZ
An Hachette UK Company

1 3 5 7 9 10 8 6 4 2

A CIP catalogue record for this book is available
from the British Library.

ISBN: 978 1 4091 6069 4

Printed in Italy

The Orion Publishing Group's policy is to use papers that are natural, renewable and recyclable
and made from wood grown in sustainable forests. The logging and manufacturing processes are
expected to conform to the environmental regulations of the country of origin.

Every effort has been made to fulfil requirements with regard to reproducing copyright material.
The author and publisher will be glad to rectify any omissions at the earliest opportunity.

www.orionbooks.co.uk

For Rupert.

Ciao Flex.

# CONTENTS

# CONTENTS

# A Song of Ice, Fire and Jam:

'I Jammy Lannister declare upon the honour of my house that my ~~beloved~~ brother left no trueborn heirs.

By right of birth, blood and dough, I do this day lay claim to the Iron Scone of Westeros. Let all men declare their loyalty.'

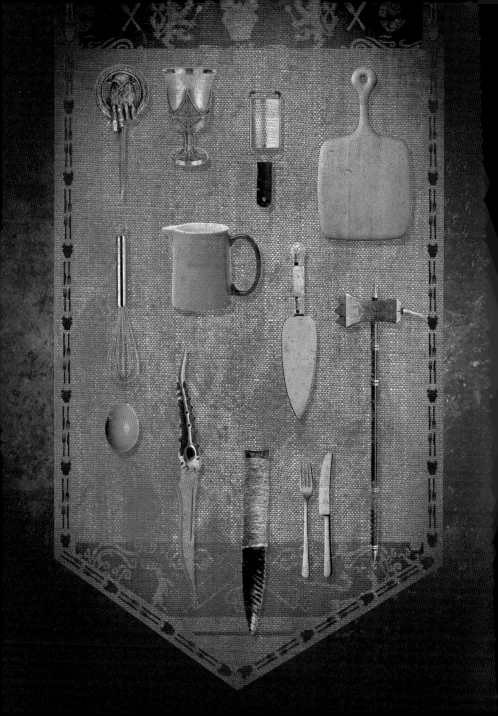

# A KITCHEN NEEDS UTENSILS AS A SWORD NEEDS A WHETSTONE

## Make sure you have everything you need to back up your claim to the Iron Scone

# YOU WIN
# OR YOU DINE.
# THERE IS NO
# MIDDLE GROUND

USE THE SEAL AND CHOOSE THE DIFFICULTY
OF YOUR BAKE WISELY...

**HARD**
'VALAR
MORGHULIS'

**MEDIUM**
'WHAT IS DEAD
MAY NEVER DIE;
BUT RISE
AGAIN STRONGER'

**EASY**
'WHY IS IT ALWAYS
THE INNOCENTS
THAT SUFFER MOST?'

DINNER
IS
COMING

# Bran Muffins

Perfect for a long journey of self-discovery, these plucky little treats are so good they're Warg-asmic!

## Ingredients

175g oat bran
200ml buttermilk
100ml sunflower oil
1 medium egg
125g demerara sugar
1 tsp vanilla extract
1 tsp baking powder
75g currants, raisins or sultanas
175g self-raising flour (only by falling can we raise ourselves up)
450g icing sugar, sifted
250g butter, softened
1-2 tbsp (15-30ml) milk, if necessary
Pink and black food colours
Large white chocolate buttons
Chocolate writing icing
1 bag liquorice strips

Feeds 5

# Directions

Line a muffin tin with paper cases. Preheat the oven to 180°C (160°C fan-assisted/350°f/Gas mark 4). In a large bowl, mix together the bran and buttermilk and allow to stand for 10 minutes (sadly, this will be the last time they ever stand).

Meanwhile, in a separate bowl, mix the oil, egg, sugar and vanilla. Do it quietly so as not to frighten Hodor.

Stir the baking powder and fruit into the flour, then combine all three mixtures until just combined: do not overmix and leave a little lumpy.

Scoop into the paper cases and bake for 15-20 minutes until risen and beginning to brown. Transfer to a rack to cool.

Beat the icing sugar and butter together until light and fluffy, adding a little milk if necessary. Divide the icing into two bowls. Add a little pink food colour to one bowl until a flesh colour is achieved, and colour the other icing grey by using a tiny amount of black colouring. Smooth the pink icing all over the top of each muffin, piling it up as necessary to make a mounded head shape. Transfer the grey icing to a piping bag with a plain nozzle and pipe on hair. Add eyes and hair to the white chocolate buttons with chocolate writing icing. Cut the liquorice strips into limbs with a sharp knife and then add them and the chocolate buttons to sit on top of the muffin head. Lastly, add eyes to the large heads using raisins cut in half.

Enjoy and watch as past, present, and future come together and make time meaningless! Although they're absolutely perfect for teatime.

# Oberyn's Smashing Surprise

An explosion of chocolate and fruit that serves
a gruesome reminder to always finish your dinner
before walking away

## Ingredients

1 punnet fresh raspberries
100g chocolate egg, about 12cm tall
1 packet strawberry or raspberry jelly
100g butter, softened
175g icing sugar, sifted
Black and red food colours
A handful of cashew nuts

Feeds 8

# DIRECTIONS

Cut the raspberries into mashed-brain-sized pieces.

Take the chocolate egg and, using a knife, cut a small hole in the top of the egg towards the back.

In a jug, make up the jelly as directed on the packet and stir in the raspberries (you should have expected this recipe to be a little fruity), putting it aside to cool.

Meanwhile, beat the butter and icing sugar together until fluffy. Keeping back a very small amount for the tongue, colour the butter cream with black food colour. Colour the remaining amount red. Transfer the black icing to a piping bag fitted with a plain nozzle and add hair and features to the egg. Fill in the tongue with the red icing using the tip of a knife.

Crush the cashew nuts using a large knife and with leftover icing, attach them to the mouth to look like teeth.

Once cooled and just beginning to set, carefully pour the jelly into the head and leave to set.

To serve, place your thumbs in the egg's 'eyes', allowing them to melt the chocolate a little before pushing through and crushing the egg to reveal the jelly inside.

As the chocolate face gives way beneath your hands, loudly confess to your hideous crimes and watch as your guests quietly make towards the door.

# DAENERYS' DRAGON EGGS
## AND
## UNSULLIED SOLDIERS
## (WITHOUT NUTS)

Why have one dragon when you can have three?
With the right combination of patience and the magic
of fire, these chocolatey miracles will leave you poised
to aggressively conquer any party

## INGREDIENTS

### FOR EACH EGG
A divine right to rule
100g chocolate egg, about 12cm tall
70g pack chocolate buttons
Edible food colour sprays
Ships. You'll need ships unfortunately

### FOR THE SOLDIERS
1 pack chocolate buttons, plus extra chocolate buttons for melting
1 pack ladyfinger sponge biscuits
1 pack chocolate sticks

*Feeds 4*

# DIRECTIONS

Stand the egg in an egg cup or other suitable container to keep it upright.

Melt the tip of each button by holding it briefly in the flame of the hob (or use a little melted chocolate). Try not to think of Daeron's head liquefying while you do this.

Starting at the bottom edge, stick evenly to the egg, working your way up and round until it is covered, overlapping each row by the next, like scales.

Chill until set, then spray with the edible food colours.

With a sharp knife, trim one button for each soldier into a helmet shape, as shown. Melt a few buttons in a small basin over hot water, or in the microwave, and stick the helmet to each biscuit with a little melted chocolate. Add a chocolate shield, then stick a chocolate spear and each soldier to a chocolate button base.

Legend has it the eggs are activated by walking them into a blazing fire – though this is a health and safety nightmare. You can just break them apart with a spoon and serve.

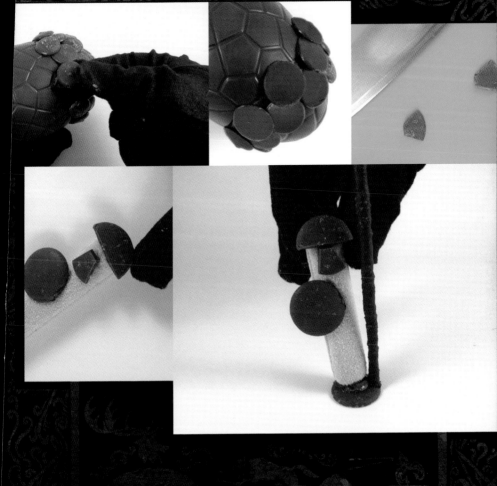

# THREE-EYED RAVEN PIES

Ominously delicious? Portentously tempting? Forebodingly moreish? Whatever you think of these weird little treats, you won't need to watch what you eat…because they'll be watching you!

## INGREDIENTS

500g ready-made shortcrust pastry
Many three-eyed ravens. Unusually for birds, look for them beneath trees in northern regions
500g pack Black Forest frozen fruits, semi-defrosted (for a more gruesome alternative, try using Children of the Forest)
A little water and caster sugar
1 medium egg yolk, lightly beaten with a little water
A few liquorice strips
Sugar eyeballs
Greensight

*Feeds 4*

# DIRECTIONS

Lightly grease the holes in a muffin tin, or spray with non-stick baking spray. Preheat the oven to 200°C/180°C fan assisted/400°f/ Gas mark 6).

Roll out the pastry on a floured work surface and, using the edge of a saucer as a guide, cut circles large enough to line the holes in the tin, with an overlap around the top edges.

Fill each pie with fruit, and sprinkle with a little water and a teaspoonful of sugar.

Sadly, three-eyed ravens tend to bring depressing news/revelations as opposed to the more common two-eyed breed who operate more of a general news service.

Re-roll the pastry trimmings and cut circles large enough to cover the pies and match the overlap of the linings. Dampen the edges and press the pastry together, then flute the edges with your fingers.

Brush the surfaces of the pies with the egg-yolk wash.

Bake for 25 minutes, then carefully remove the pies from the tin. Place on a baking tray and bake for a further 5-10 minutes to firm up the pastry cases.

Trim the liquorice strips to beak-like shapes with a sharp knife. Make a small hole in the top of each pie and add a beak. Dampen the sugar eyes with a little water until sticky, and add three to each pie.

Realise that the bird is actually an old man who has a thousand eyes but only one; who is what he is but is also what he isn't. Enjoy a pie warm from the oven while you contemplate the mystery of it all.

# FEED ME MORE!

# Weirwood Tree-eats

Bend your knee and swear an oath to this most sacred of snacks – whether you follow the Old Gods or bask in the light of the Seven, this cupcake will make you a true believer

## Ingredients

100g butter, softened
100g caster sugar
2 medium eggs
125g self-raising flour
1 tsp baking powder
few drops strawberry essence or flavouring
Pink food colour

### TO DECORATE
125g icing sugar, sifted
25g butter
60g cream cheese
150g white chocolate drops
Dried strawberry pieces
A little extra icing sugar, for dusting
1 tube red writing icing

*Feeds 6*

# DIRECTIONS

Preheat the oven to 180°C (160°C fan assisted/350°F/Gas mark 4).
Place 6 large paper cases into a muffin or bun tin.

Any wight friends of yours will have to leave the party.

Put all the cake ingredients into a mixing bowl except the food colouring and
beat well together, first with a wooden spoon, then with a whisk until properly
mixed and smooth, adding the food colour gradually until a strong pink is
obtained.

With an ice-cream scoop or large spoon, divide the mix among the paper cases
and bake for 15-20 minutes until the tops are golden. Transfer to a rack to
cool completely before decorating.

Beat the icing sugar and butter together in a free-standing electric mixer with
a paddle attachment on medium-slow speed until they come together and are
well mixed.

Add the cream cheese in one go and beat until it is completely incorporated.
Turn the mixer up to medium-high speed. Continue beating for at least 5
minutes until light and fluffy. Spoon or pipe the cream cheese icing on top of
the cold cakes.

Melt the white chocolate very gently over hot water. Transfer to a piping bag
with a small plain nozzle and pipe the tree shapes onto the paper. Carefully
add strawberry pieces to the branches and use the red writing icing to make
the trees' faces, then chill until firm.

Remove the trees from the fridge, peel carefully off the paper and push gently
into the cakes. Press a few strawberry pieces into the cupcake icing. Dust the
trees and cakes with a little sifted icing sugar.

Once finished, take a moment alone with your treats to sit in their shade and
contemplate all the bloodshed that has come before and is yet to come.

# JAMMY LANNISTER

Subject to a shockingly tasty act of mutilation, these treats somehow still manage to come in handy at tea-time

## INGREDIENTS

280g plain flour
200g firm butter, cut into small pieces (on a tree stump)
100g icing sugar
2 medium egg yolks
1 tsp vanilla extract

### TO DECORATE
Strawberry jam
Small quantity white ready to roll icing
Brown, green and black food colours
100g icing sugar, plus extra for dusting
1 medium egg white

### YOU WILL NEED
1 gingerbread man cutter

Feeds 2

# DIRECTIONS

Line a large baking tray with non-stick baking paper.

Put the flour in a bowl and add the butter. Mix till it begins to come together. Knead lightly with floured hands into a smooth dough.

Add the sugar, egg yolks and vanilla extract and mix to a dough. Put into a plastic bag and chill for at least 30 minutes.

Roll out the cookie dough on a lightly floured surface to about a 5mm thickness. Cut out shapes with the gingerbread man cutter and place them on the prepared baking tray. Cut the 'right' hands off all of them and cut mouths out of half of them with a tiny round cutter. Put back into the fridge to chill again for 30 minutes.

Meanwhile, preheat the oven to 180°C (160°C fan assisted/350°f/Gas mark 4). Bake the cookies for 12-15 minutes, until beginning to brown around the edges. Remove from the oven and allow to cool on the tray before carefully lifting off.

Sandwich the men together in pairs, one with a mouth and one without, with strawberry jam.

Cut pairs of eyes from the ready to roll icing and set aside. Knead a little brown colouring into the remaining icing. Roll out the brown icing on a surface lightly dusted with icing sugar and cut out hair, beards and moustaches. Stick to the heads with mouths with a little water.

Sieve the icing sugar into a small bowl and add some egg white, little by little, beating well until a piping consistency is reached. Divide into two and colour one half green and the other black. With a piping bag fitted with a small plain nozzle (or small paper piping bag with the end cut off), pipe the outline of the jackets in black. Loosen the texture of the green icing with some water, then carefully fill the jacket shapes using a small teaspoon. Allow to set.

Stick the eyes to the heads with a little water. Add the pupils with the black colouring and jam to the cut-off hands, all the while screaming in horror and swearing revenge. You do, after all, always pay your debts.

# ARYA
# HUNGRY?

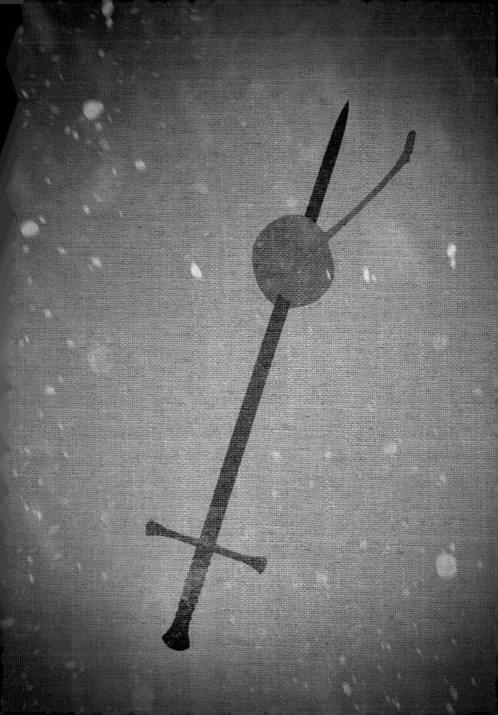

# Hot Pie's Wolfbread

A recipe that improves every time you make it, this delicious doughy direwolf is a perfect gift for homesick friends

## Ingredients

275ml warm water
45ml sunflower oil
2 tbsp liquid honey
500g wholemeal bread flour
1½ tsp fast-action dried yeast
Pinch salt

Feeds 5

# DIRECTIONS

Mix the warm water, sunflower oil and honey in a large mixing bowl. Place the remaining ingredients together in a small bowl, stir together and add to the wet ingredients. Mix together until a sticky dough is formed, then turn out onto a lightly floured surface and knead well for 20-30 minutes until the dough is elastic and springy to the touch. (Or use the dough hook in an electric mixer.)

Cover the dough with a clean tea towel and leave in a warm place to rise until doubled in size.

Turn out onto a lightly floured surface and knead again briefly. Roll out with a well-floured rolling pin and cut out wolf shapes. (Any leftover dough can be shaped into balls, for bread rolls.) Place on a lightly greased baking tray.

Leave for half an hour or so to rise again, then put in the oven preheated to 220°C (200°C fan assisted/425°f/Gas mark 7). Turn down the heat to 200°C (180°C fan assisted/400°f/Gas mark 6) and bake for 15-20 minutes until browning around the edges.

Entrust your vulpine masterpiece to a travelling knight in the hope it will reach your friend and offer them some consolation for the violent deaths of many of their immediate family.

# Joffrey's Jaffa Poison Cup

Some puddings just have it coming to them.
And as much as no-one wants to be a king-slayer,
who cares when revenge tastes this sweet?

## Ingredients

### FOR THE GOBLET
A cardboard centre of a loo roll
A saucer
Gold edible food spray
A bowl
Edible glue
1 pack boiled sweets

### FOR THE FILLING
1 packet orange jelly
300ml double cream
Black and red food colours
Large white chocolate buttons
Strawberry 'laces'
A dose of 'the strangler'

Feeds 4

# DIRECTIONS

for the goblet, place the loo roll on top of the saucer and spray gold. Separately spray the bowl and use the edible glue to attach the boiled sweet gems.

Use edible glue to affix the bowl to the loo roll.

Once the goblet is dry and firm, make up the jelly as directed on the packet and allow to cool. Pour into the goblet and chill for a few hours or overnight until set.

Whip the cream to soft peak stage, then spread carefully over the surface of the jelly, smoothing it with a dampened knife.

Paint a little red food colour around the edges of the chocolate drops and add pupils to the centres with the black colour. Place on the cream and add strawberry lace 'veins', cutting them as necessary.

Wait for the dwarfs' re-enactment to finish – you don't want to be rude.

It's time to dish out (just) desserts.

# OURS
# IS THE
# FOODIE

# Castle Black Forest Gateau

A legendary dessert that has stood the test of time (a hundred generations to be exact). Do you have what it takes to keep it together?

## Ingredients

300g butter, softened
400g sugar
6 medium eggs, lightly beaten (if you can't take a beating, this isn't the cake for you)
2 tsp vanilla extract
350g self-raising flour
100g cocoa powder, sifted
90ml milk
350ml double or whipping cream
1 jar black cherry compote or jam
3-4 tbsp (45-60ml) Kirsch
1-2 packs chocolate sticks
Icing sugar, to finish
An absolute load of cold-rolled steel

Feeds 8

# DIRECTIONS

Preheat the oven to 180°C (160°C fan assisted/350°F/Gas mark 4).
Grease and line a 34cm x 23cm deep rectangular baking tin.

Cream the butter and sugar until pale in colour, light and fluffy. Add the eggs
very gradually, beating well between each addition. Stir in the vanilla extract.
Combine the flour and cocoa powder, then fold into the mix until blended.
Add enough milk to give a dropping consistency and spoon into the prepared
tin, smoothing the top and making a slight dip in the centre.

Bake for 45-55 minutes, or until firm to the touch and a knife inserted in the
centre comes out clean (like a human sword passing through a White Walker).
Cool in the tin for a few minutes, then turn out onto a rack to cool completely
while you wait for Stannis to arrive.

Cut about a quarter off one end of the cake. Whip the cream to soft peak stage
and spread about half all over the top and sides of the larger piece. Chill while
you construct the castle.

Cut the remaining piece of cake in half horizontally and sandwich together
again with cream and some of the cherry compote or jam. Chill to firm up.
Cut shapes to make the castle as shown, sandwiching them to different
heights with more jam and cream and cutting sloping sections for the roofs.
Spoon a little Kirsch over the individual 'buildings'. Add chocolate sticks to
top the roofs and to form entrances. Dust the buildings with a little sifted
icing sugar.

Add a chocolate stick ladder to the 'wall'. Carefully stand the wall on one
edge (leaning it against a suitable prop if necessary) and add the castle
buildings at the base.

Once cooked and coated, the wall will stand… With me now! Now with me!

# Tyrion's Shortbread

*A very small biscuit that casts a very large shadow...*

## Ingredients

100g butter, softened
50g caster sugar
150g plain flour
25g cornflour
1 medium egg white
125g icing sugar, sifted
Yellow, black, blue, brown, red and purple food colours
Tiny quantity ready to roll white icing, for eyes

## YOU WILL NEED

1 'gingerbread man' cutter
1 x 6cm round cutter
7,800 jars of wildfire

*Feeds 2*

# DIRECTIONS

Preheat the oven to 170°C (150°C fan assisted/325°f/Gas mark 3). Line a large baking tray with non-stick baking paper. Cream the butter and sugar together in a mixing bowl with a wooden spoon until creamy, like Shae's soft, soft skin. Mix together the flour and cornflour and add it to the butter/sugar, encouraging it to blend in with the back of the spoon.

Turn the lumpy mix out onto a work surface or silicone sheet dusted with flour, and work the dough gently with your hands until it comes together (don't overdo it or the dough will become oily and tough). Ask friends for help if necessary: Bronn, perhaps, if Jaime isn't to hand. Wrap and chill for at least an hour.

Dust the work surface and a rolling pin well with flour and roll out the dough very gently, pushing it together with your hands as cracks form. Cut shapes with a gingerbread man cutter. Using a 6cm round cutter, cut and add large heads to the bodies by pressing gently together, using a little water to stick if necessary. (Bake the cut off heads to nibble separately.)

Place on the prepared tray and bake for 20-25 minutes or until just beginning to brown around the edges. Allow to cool on a rack.

Prepare the royal icing by lightly whisking the egg white in a cup. Place the sifted icing sugar in a mixing bowl and add the egg white, little by little, beating between each addition with a wooden spoon until a piping consistency is achieved (you will probably not need all of the egg white).

Divide the icing into 3 cups and colour the different amounts black, yellow and purple. Place the black into a small piping bag with a plain nozzle and pipe the outline of jackets and trousers. Add a little water to the purple icing and spoon into the jacket shapes. Add a little water to the remaining black icing and spoon it into the trousers. Place the yellow icing in a bag with a plain nozzle and pipe on hair. Add a tiny amount of brown colour to the remaining yellow icing and add eyebrows. Paint on a scar with red colour. Add piped on black nostrils and mouth. Add tiny ready to roll icing eyes and paint on irises and pupils with the blue and black colours.

Don't expect anyone to show gratitude for this diminutive delight. Often overlooked, if not outright despised, it takes a more subtle mind to appreciate its hidden depths.

# Nedible Stark and Traitor's Walk Treats

These 'severed Neds' are best eaten with 'the hand' – be sure to consume them quickly, as they won't last as long as you'd hope

## Ingredients

400g milk chocolate, in drops or broken into pieces
350g Madeira cake or any basic sponge cake, chocolate or plain,
   blitzed in a food processor
175g white chocolate, in drops or chopped into pieces
A few drops pink or paprika food colour
Cola laces and chocolate sprinkles, to decorate
Edible glue
1 tube black writing icing
Black and red food colours
180g rice crispies
45g butter
454g tub Marshmallow fluff
A generous amount of honour but not much common sense

### YOU WILL NEED
1 or 2 cake pop moulds and cake pop sticks
Wooden skewers

Feeds 8

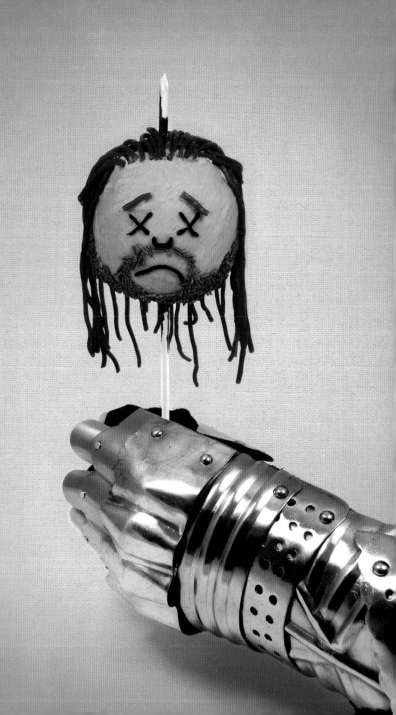

# DIRECTIONS

Melt 350g of the milk chocolate very gently in a bowl over hot water, stirring occasionally until just melted. Add the cake crumbs to the melted chocolate and stir well until mixed. Press into a cake pop mould (or shape with your hands). Freeze for 10 minutes.

Shape a large 'Ned' with your hands. Place the large head on a small piece of non-stick baking paper and freeze.

To coat with chocolate: melt the white chocolate very gently, then add a tiny amount of pink or paprika food colour to make a flesh colour.

Unmould the cake pop heads. Insert a wooden skewer or cake pop stick into each head and dip the cold heads in the chocolate, rolling them around to coat, and place them back in the freezer for a few moments to firm up. Coat 'Ned' in the same way.

Add cola lace hair and eyebrows to Ned, sticking with a little melted chocolate. Using edible glue, add a chocolate sprinkle beard and moustache. Add black writing icing eyes, nose and mouth.

Paint features on the small heads with black food colour. Melt the remaining milk chocolate as before, and pipe on hair, beards and moustaches. Add red blood with food colour.

Keep the heads in a cool place while you make the 'wall'.

Crush the rice crispies in a plastic bag with a rolling pin. Melt the butter in a saucepan over low heat and stir in 300g of the Marshmallow Fluff. Stir well until completely melted. Add the crushed cereal and stir well. Press into a small greased baking tray and allow to cool.

Cut bricks out of the cold mixture. Assemble some of the bricks into a round turret with the remaining Marshmallow Fluff. Fill the centre with the remaining cereal bricks, pressing them down as necessary to make a firm base. Push the heads into the base and add chocolate sprinkles to cover the centre.

Grab a knife and prepare to serve – and remember: 'He who passes the sentence should swing the knife'.

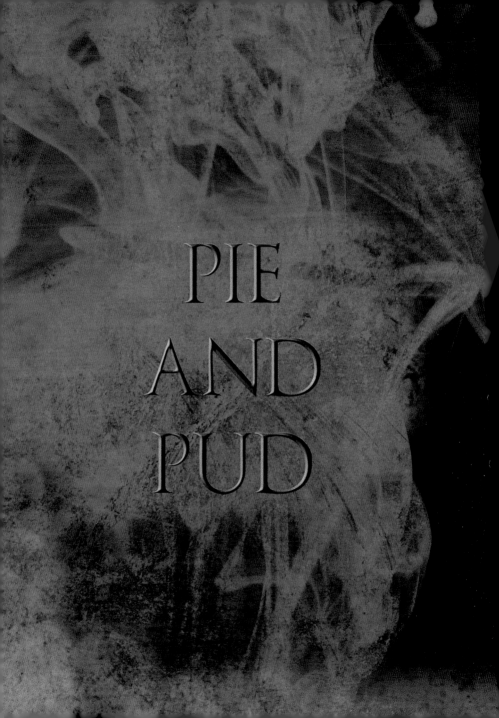

# PIE

# AND

# PUD

# White Walker Walnut Whip

Winter is coming. And what better way to while away the Long Night than with these ungodly treats?

## Ingredients

200g dark chocolate
Marshmallow fluff
Blue hard-shelled chocolates
Blue food colour
4-5 chocolate sticks
Blue hard-boiled sweets
4-5 walnut halves
Newborn male children

### FOR THE BABIES

Jelly babies
Pink ready to roll icing
Blue sugar drops

### YOU WILL NEED

1 gingerbread man cutter

Feeds 2

# Directions

Clear the work surface of any dragon glass.

Melt the chocolate in a bowl over a saucepan of hot water on the stove. Once it is melted and smooth, tip out onto non-stick baking paper and spread evenly and smoothly with a palette knife. Allow to cool. Once cooled and hardened, use a gingerbread man cutter to make four or five men. Keep any leftover chocolate to re-melt later for sticking.

Spoon the Marshmallow fluff into a large piping bag with a plain nozzle. Pipe the outline of each man onto a chocolate shape as shown, then fill in the centre. When set, add blue chocolate eyes and add pupils and other details with the blue food colour and melted chocolate.

Wrap each jelly baby head in a tiny piece of icing and stick on blue sugar drop eyes with a little water. Stick a piece of blue sweet to each chocolate stick with a little melted chocolate.

Stick a chocolate spear, baby and walnut half to each man with a little melted chocolate.

Place the blue-eyed baby on a home-made altar and let shriek a battle cry to let your guests know tea is ready.

# Littlefinger Cake

*A truly Baelish-ious dessert that will sweet-talk you into your guests' favour*

## Ingredients

1 pack ladyfinger sponge biscuits
2-3 tbsp (30-45ml) rum, brandy or fruit juice
3 medium eggs
175g caster sugar
Juice and grated zest of 2 medium-sized
   unwaxed lemons
3 tsp powdered gelatine
100ml boiling water
300ml double cream
Cocoa powder
1 small pack blanched almonds
A network of spies throughout the kingdom
   and a low moral threshold

YOU WILL NEED
20cm springform cake tin

Feeds 8

# DIRECTIONS

Line the base of a 20cm springform cake tin with enough sponge fingers to cover, trimming as necessary. Sprinkle the rum/brandy/fruit juice over and allow to soak in for a few minutes. Line the side of the tin with the remaining fingers, pushing them into the soft sponge base to help them to stay upright.

Separate the eggs, putting the yolks into a large mixing bowl together with the caster sugar, and placing the whites into a separate bowl to whisk later.

Whisk the yolks and sugar with an electric mixer or by hand until they are thickened slightly, pale and fluffy. Add the lemon juice and zest and whisk together.

Place the powdered gelatine in a small bowl and add the boiling water. Stir well until the powder is dissolved and allow to cool for a couple of minutes before adding to the yolk mixture.

In another bowl, beat the cream until thick and softly peaking, then fold into the yolk mixture.

In another bowl, whisk the egg whites stiffly and fold gently into the yolk/cream mixture until blended.

Spoon or pour into the lined cake tin and smooth the top, keeping back a tiny amount to stick on nails later. Chill for a few hours or overnight until firm.

Cut a paper stencil of a bird shape as shown. Place carefully on top of the mousse, then sift cocoa powder over the top. Remove the paper. Cut the almonds in half and stick one to each 'finger' with the kept back mousse.

Just before serving, carefully remove the outside of the tin. Serve on the tin base, as the rum-soaked biscuit base will be very soft.

Serve and enjoy. Any guests who aren't adequately appreciative can be shown the (moon) door.

# Sansa's Lemon Cakes

A refined and noble treat, favoured by the upper classes, these courtly delights are best served with a side of intrigue and a thin veneer of respectability

## Ingredients

### FOR THE CAKES

5 medium eggs
225g butter, softened
225g icing sugar, sifted
225g plain flour
1 rounded tsp baking powder
Grated zest of 1 unwaxed lemon (you will need to import
   these from Dorne, so they are likely to be expensive)
1-2 tbsp (15-30ml) milk, if necessary

### FOR THE ICING

50g icing sugar, sifted
1 medium egg white, lightly beaten
Juice of ½ lemon
Red and black edible food spray
Gold ribbon

### YOU WILL NEED

Firm paper or card
1 scalpel

Feeds 4

# Directions

Preheat the oven to 180°C (160°C fan assisted/350°F/Gas mark 4). Grease a 23cm round baking tin and line the bottom with non-stick baking paper.

Put all the cake ingredients except the milk into a large mixing bowl and beat well until blended. Ask Joffrey to give you a hand with the beating. Add a little milk, as necessary, to give a 'dropping' consistency.

Spoon into the prepared tin and bake for 25-30 minutes, or until firm to the touch and a knife inserted in the centre comes out clean. Why not kill some time with a return journey to Traitor's Walk to look at your father's impaled head?

Allow to cool for a few minutes in the tin, before turning out onto a rack to cool completely.

Cut out little cakes using a 6cm round cutter. Trim to the cutter's edge using a knife so the cakes are a uniform height.

Add the egg white little by little to the icing sugar, beating well between each addition, until the texture is smooth but still thick. Add the lemon juice, gradually, until a flowing texture is achieved. Pour over the tops of the cakes and spread with a knife, as necessary, to cover the surfaces.

Allow to set in a cool place for a few hours until the surface is dry and hard. Draw outlines of the Stark and Lannister sigils onto a piece of firm paper or card and cut out the centres carefully, using a scalpel, to make stencils.

One by one, place a stencil on the top of each cake and spray carefully with the edible food sprays. Attach a piece of ribbon around each cake, sticking the ends with a little icing.

Enjoy the lemony goodness and try to avoid getting married again any time soon.

FILLET.

JUICY.

HADDOCK.

# BRIENNE OF TART

Can you BEAR to resist this custardy concoction?
One bite and your guests will swear oaths to
you forever

## INGREDIENTS

350g ready-made shortcrust pastry
8 medium egg yolks
100g caster sugar
1 tsp vanilla extract
250ml milk
250ml double cream
freshly grated nutmeg
1 pack chocolate sticks

Feeds 8

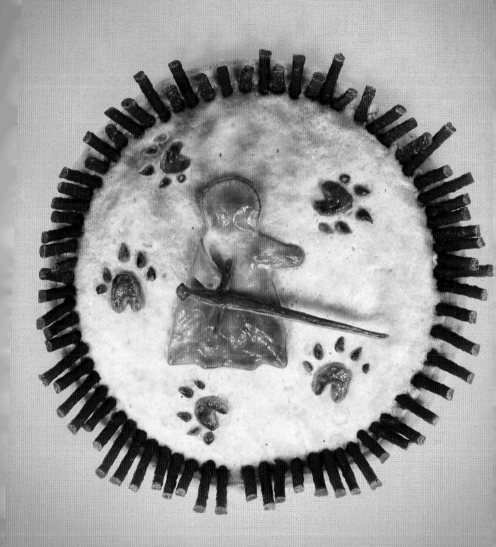

# DIRECTIONS

On a lightly floured surface, roll out the pastry and line a greased and floured loose-bottomed 27cm flan tin, leaving an overlap round the edges, keeping back any pastry trimmings to make the decorations later. Prick the base with a fork and chill for 30 minutes.

Preheat the oven to 180°C (160°C fan assisted/350°f/Gas mark 4). Put a circle of baking paper or silicone into the base of the flan and fill it with baking beans. Bake for 20 minutes, then remove the beans and lining paper and cook for about 15 minutes more.

Remove the flan from the oven and turn down the heat to 140°C (120°C fan assisted/275°f/Gas mark 1). Trim the surplus pastry off the top edge of the flan.

Keeping back a tiny amount of egg yolk for later, beat the yolks, caster sugar and vanilla extract together until pale, thick and fluffy. Put the milk and cream into a saucepan together with a little grated nutmeg and bring to the boil, then pour it over the yolk/sugar mixture, stirring well all the time. Strain into a jug, then leave for a few minutes for any foam to rise to the top.

Skim any foam off the top of the custard and pour carefully into the pastry case, keeping any left over to hand. Bake for about 40-50 minutes, topping up as necessary with any leftover custard, until almost completely set. Cut the chocolate sticks into different lengths and arrange around the edge of the tart.

Leave to cool completely, then use the kept-back pastry to cut out shapes for Brienne, her sword and the bear prints. With a fork, mix the remaining egg yolk with a small amount of water and brush lightly over the shapes. Line a large baking sheet with non-stick baking paper, add the shapes and bake in the oven for about 15 minutes. Place the shapes onto the top of the tart.

Devour in man-sized bites.

# Sigil Snacks

Which house is truly the greatest? It's time to find out once and for all with these delicious treats for feuding foodies

## Ingredients

280g plain flour
200g firm butter, cut into pieces
100g icing sugar
2 medium egg yolks
1 tsp vanilla extract
Red, black, blue, yellow and green paste food colours
3-4 brightly coloured boiled sweets
Hundreds of years of murder, incest and ruthless ambition

### YOU WILL NEED

1 7cm round cutter
1 scalpel

*Feeds 5*

# Directions

Put the flour in a bowl and add the butter. Rub the butter into the flour with your fingertips until the mix looks like breadcrumbs.

Add the sugar, egg yolks and vanilla extract and mix to a dough. Knead lightly, then divide the dough into five, colouring each one by kneading the five paste colours into it, adding little by little until the right depth of colour is achieved. Place in separate food bags and chill for at least 30 minutes. Line a large baking tray with non-stick baking paper.

Roll out each piece of dough on a lightly floured work surface and cut rounds with a 7cm round cutter, cutting a couple of red and blue rounds in half and re-joining them to make two half-red half-blue biscuits. Cut shapes out of the centres as shown, using a scalpel. For comprehensive knowledge of the houses, you will need access to the Great Library at Harrenhal. Place the biscuits on the prepared tray and chill again for 30 minutes.

Meanwhile, preheat the oven to 180°C (160°C fan assisted/350°F/Gas mark 4). Place the differently coloured boiled sweets into individual plastic food bags and crush very finely with a rolling pin.

Bake the cookies for 8-10 minutes until a little risen. Remove from the oven. Fill the shapes in the middle with the crushed sweets, easing them into the corners with a cocktail stick or similar. Carefully brush any excess off the cookies. Return to the oven for 3-4 minutes, until the crushed sugar is melted and the cookies are beginning to brown around the edges. Remove from the oven and allow to cool on the tray before carefully lifting off.

Remember that power resides where men believe it resides, it is just a shadow on the wall, blah blah... just eat the biscuits.

# Jaime and Cersei's Family Mess

Take some meringue, some strawberries and some cream, add a whole lot of incestuous lovin' and you've got yourself a party, Lannister style!

## Ingredients

2 medium egg whites
100g caster sugar
1 tsp white wine vinegar
Blue and black food colours
White chocolate buttons

### For the Eton Mess
300ml double cream
1 large punnet ripe strawberries

### You Will Need
1 gingerbread man cutter

Feeds 6

# DIRECTIONS

Draw round a gingerbread man cutter to create the outline of four to six men and a small sword onto non-stick baking paper. Place onto one or two large baking trays.

Preheat the oven to 110°C (95°C fan assisted/225°f/Gas mark ¼).

Whisk the egg whites until very stiff.

Add the sugar and vinegar and whisk again, until it's almost as stiff as before. Put the meringue mix into a large piping bag fitted with a plain nozzle and pipe onto the shapes on the paper.

Bake for about 3-4 hours, turning the oven down even further if the meringues begin to brown. Once the meringues can be loosened from the paper, they are ready to come out of the oven.

Remove from the oven, extract the meringues from the paper and cool on a rack.

Whip the cream to soft peak stage and spoon it into a shallow dish. Keeping back four or five whole strawberries, slice the rest thinly and arrange on top of the cream, overlapping as necessary to cover the surface. Trim the ends off the whole strawberries and use them to form Joffrey's berth. Add the meringue characters (you can pick out the best three) and the sword to the top of the strawberries. Apply blue and black food colours to the chocolate buttons with a paintbrush to create Joffrey's eyes.

To turn it into the Eton Mess, simply break up the meringue into small pieces, then mash them together with the strawberries and cream with a fork. Serve chilled.

Eat in the privacy of your own home, chapel or tower and toss any witnesses out of the window as necessary.

WE
DO
SOY

# Red (Velvet) Wedding Cake

This deliciously bloodthirsty cake makes a wedding gift to die for, though some may find it hard to stomach…

## Ingredients

### FOR THE CAKES:
1.15kg butter, softened
1.15kg caster sugar
18 medium eggs, lightly beaten
2 tsp vanilla extract
1kg self-raising flour
150g cocoa powder, sifted
2 pinches salt
2 tbsp (30ml) baking powder
10-11 tbsp (165ml) red paste food colour

### FOR THE BUTTERCREAM:
750g butter, softened
1.8kg icing sugar, sifted
225g cream cheese
1 tsp vanilla extract

### FOR THE BLOOD, FIGURES AND ROSES:
250g white ready to roll icing
Small amount brown ready to roll icing
Black, pink and red food colours
2 medium egg whites
350-500g icing sugar
1 tsp glycerine

### FOR THE DIREWOLF, ARROWS AND SWORD:
Chocolate sticks
1 packet strawberry astro belts
Melted chocolate, for gluing
1 Refresher or similar hard candy bar
Silver edible food spray
1 Crunchie bar
1 hard-boiled sweet
A small quantity of cake pop mix - see page 59
2 Rolos
Chocolate icing for decoration
2 chocolate drops

### TO ICE:
2.5kg white ready to roll icing

### YOU WILL NEED
1 x 15cm round cake tin
1 x 23cm round cake tin
1 x 30cm round cake tin, all around 7.5cm depth
6 or 7 musically capable assassins
1 x 15cm cake board
1 x 23cm cake board
1 x 36cm cake board
8 plastic cake dowels

Feeds 8

# DIRECTIONS

The Lannisters send their regards…

For the cake: Grease and line a 15cm, a 23cm and a 30cm cake tin, all around 7.5cm deep, with non-stick baking paper. Preheat the oven to 180°C (160°C fan assisted/350°F/Gas mark 4). You may need to do this in batches as it makes a large quantity and won't all fit in one bowl at once. Cream the butter and sugar together until light and fluffy, then gradually add the eggs, together with the vanilla extract, beating between every addition. In a separate bowl, mix together the flour, cocoa powder, salt and baking powder. Fold the flour mix into the egg and sugar, then stir in the red colour and mix well.

Transfer to the prepared tins and bake for the following times:
Small tier – 30-40 mins
Medium tier – 65-75 mins
Large tier – 75 -85 mins.

The cakes are ready when risen and firm and a knife inserted in the centres comes out clean. Allow each to cool in their tin for a few minutes, then turn out onto a rack to cool completely. Remove the paper carefully.

To make the buttercream: Beat together the softened butter and icing sugar until light and fluffy. Add the cream cheese and a few drops of vanilla extract and beat again.

Cut the cakes in half horizontally with a long-bladed serrated knife and sandwich them together again with buttercream. Stick each to a cake board with a little buttercream, then spread a layer of buttercream over the tops and sides. Chill until this sets, then spread the remaining buttercream in a thin layer over the cakes to give a flat finish.

Measure over the top and sides of each cake and roll out and cut a circle of the ready to roll icing to this diameter. Lift over the cake and smooth with your hands, trimming around the bottom edge as necessary.

(Continued overleaf.)

# Directions continued

Hold a dowel at the side of the largest cake and mark with a pencil where it is level with the icing - it mustn't stick up. Cut the rod and three others to the same length. Push the rods into the cake about 5cm in from the edge of the cake, evenly spaced in a square formation. Repeat for the medium-sized cake. Stack the cakes one on top of each other.

For the arrows, use chocolate sticks with strips of astro belts cut to look like feathers affixed with a small amount of melted chocolate. For the sword, spray a Refresher or hard candy bar silver and fix to half a Crunchie with melted chocolate, adding a boiled sweet to decorate.

The direwolf uses the cake pop recipe from 'Nedible Starks' earlier in the book, with half a Rolo for the snout and each ear and chocolate icing to cover. The eyes are made from chocolate drops.

To make the roses: Keeping back a little for the figures, knead the white icing until soft. For each rose, make a small cone shape and stand it on the work surface. Roll little balls of icing and flatten into petal shapes before sticking to the cone with a little water. Build up the rose by adding petals of increasing size. Finally, twist off the surplus icing at the base.

For the figures: Colour the remaining white icing pink, by kneading in a tiny amount of colour. Make simple heads and bodies, then 'dress' them in scraps of brown icing. Paint on features with black colour. Make a tiny knife with icing painted black.

For the blood: Lightly beat the egg whites in a large bowl. Add the sieved icing sugar, little by little, beating well until a thick pouring consistency is achieved. Beat in the glycerine to add gloss, then add red colour until the icing looks 'blood-like'.

When fully assembled, pour the 'blood' all over the cakes, as if emanating from the slashed throat of the kneeling figure.

Once that's done, sit back and wait for 'The Rains of Castamere' to play. Then it's party time!

stay

connected

send

a raven

# Jon Snow's Crow-nut

This bastard of a dish suffers from an identity crisis: is it a croissant or a doughnut? Does it matter, though? When the outcome tastes this good, sometimes it's best to know nothing

## Ingredients

1 ½ tsp (7ml) fast-action dried yeast
100ml warm water
1 tsp (5ml) salt
2 tbsp (30ml) caster sugar
100ml milk
30g butter, melted
1 tsp (5ml) vanilla extract
1 large egg
Pinch grated nutmeg
170g butter, very soft (the Wall will toughen it up)
Cooking oil (virgin, ideally, but that's easier said than done)
250g icing sugar, sifted
Pink and black food colours
Chocolate sprinkles
1 medium egg white

Feeds 2

# DIRECTIONS

Sprinkle the yeast onto the warm water and leave for 5-7 minutes until a froth appears on the surface.

Place the salt, caster sugar, milk, melted butter, vanilla extract, egg and nutmeg in a large mixing bowl. Pour in the yeast mixture and stir until it begins to form a dough. Turn out onto a lightly floured surface and knead briefly – NOT too much or the dough will be hard to handle, like Ser Alliser on a bad day.

Wrap and chill for 20-30 minutes. Winter is coming, so this shouldn't take too long.

Roll out the dough to a rectangle roughly 22cm x 45cm and roughly 5mm thick. Spread the centre third with half of the very soft butter. Fold up the bottom third of the dough to cover. Spread this portion with the remaining butter and cover with the remaining top third of the dough. Cover with cling film and a tea towel and chill for 30 minutes.

Re-roll to a rectangle about 20cm x 35cm. Fold into thirds, then roll again. Fold into thirds and roll a second time. Fold into thirds. Cover as before and chill for 2 hours. (You haven't rolled around this much since you first met Ygritte.)

Roll out to about 10mm thick. Cut out circles with a 7cm cutter, then cut holes with 2.5cm cutter. Transfer to two baking sheets lined with non-stick baking paper. Cover lightly with a tea towel and leave somewhere warm for 1 hour or until doubled in size.

Heat the cooking oil in a large pan to 175°C (350°F). Fry two Crow-nuts at a time until golden (about 1½-2 minutes each side). As you watch them burn, cry manfully, knowing that this is the only thing you've ever loved.

Allow the Crow-nuts to cool completely on a rack. Mix 125g of the icing sugar with a little warm water and pink food colour until soft. Spread over the cool doughnuts and dip the bottom halves in chocolate sprinkles. Lightly beat the egg white in a small bowl and add the remaining icing sugar and black colour to reach a piping consistency. Spoon into a piping bag with a plain nozzle and add hair and features.

# THE IRON SCONE

Forged from the remains of a thousand vanquished treats, this is the dessert to rule them all

## INGREDIENTS

225g self-raising flour
Pinch salt
¼ tsp bicarbonate of soda
50g cool butter, cut into pieces
25g caster sugar
50g of one of the following: currants, raisins, sultanas or mixed fruit
50ml milk
Whipped double cream
Strawberry jam
Chocolate finger biscuits
Mikado King chocolate biscuits
Silver edible food spray

Feeds 3

# DIRECTIONS

Preheat the oven to 200°C (180°C fan assisted/400°f/Gas mark 6), and put a large baking sheet in to get hot (no need to grease or line). For more spectacular results, use the breath of the greatest dragon.

Put the flour, salt and bicarbonate into a bowl and add the butter. Rub the butter in until the mix is like breadcrumbs.

Stir in the sugar and the fruit, if using.

Make a well in the middle and stir in enough of the milk to give a fairly soft dough.

Turn the dough out onto a floured work surface or silicone sheet and knead very lightly if necessary, just to take out any cracks.

Roll out very gently (or pat out with your hand) to about 2.5cm thick.

Cut two to three large scones with a 7cm round cutter. Sprinkle the tops with a little extra flour and put them onto the hot baking sheet.

Bake for 12-15 minutes, or until well risen and the tops are brown. Cool on a rack and serve split, with whipped cream and strawberry jam.

Shape some chocolate fingers into chisels with a sharp knife. Spray them and the Mikados with silver food colour and allow to dry. Push a bunch into each scone.

Stand back and admire in the light of the Seven. Keep away from others… The Iron Scone can NEVER be shared.

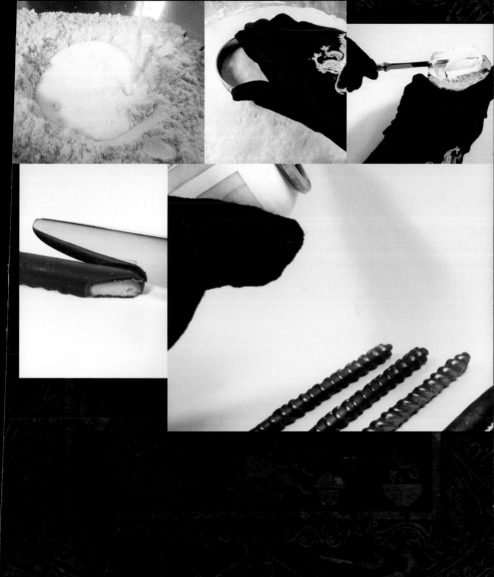

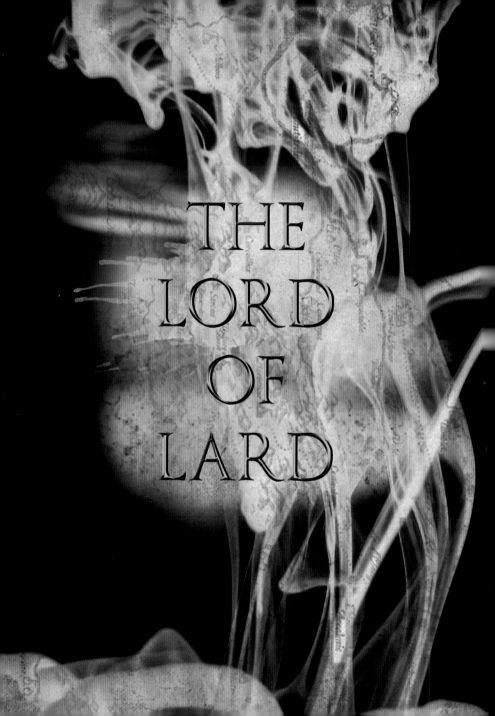

# THE
# LORD
# OF
# LARD

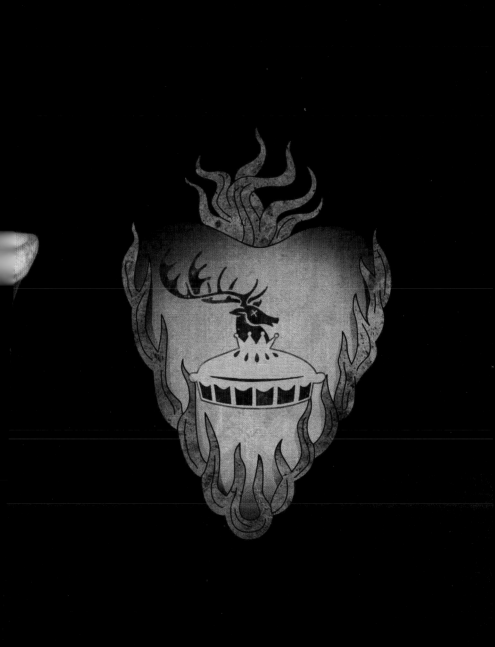

# Jaqen's Chocolate Coins

Speak the name and a man will make a snack

## Ingredients

200g chocolate drops
Pack of plain biscuits (the smoother the better)
Gold and silver edible food sprays

*Feeds 2*

# DIRECTIONS

Melt the chocolate over hot water or in the microwave. Pour a little chocolate over one side of each biscuit and spread with a palette knife. Put a small amount of chocolate into a piping bag with small plain nozzle and pipe the outlines of the symbols and figures onto the biscuits, using two biscuits to represent both sides of the coin. Using a teaspoon, flood chocolate into the outline of the figure's hood.

'Valar Morghulis', you're nearly there.

Once the chocolate is cold and hard, spray with the coloured food spray.

Use any leftover icing and spray on your face to effect a total transformation and terrify nearby children.

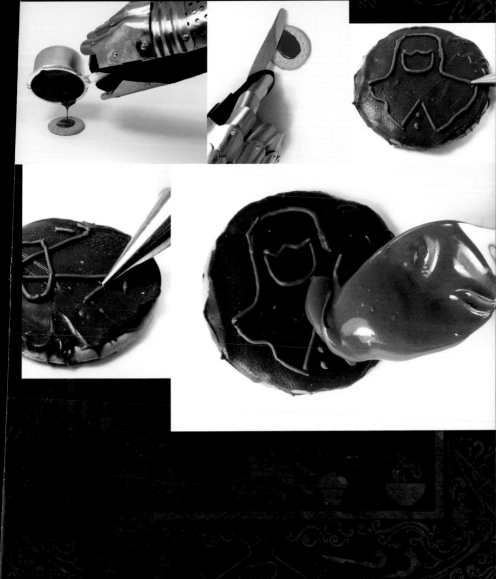

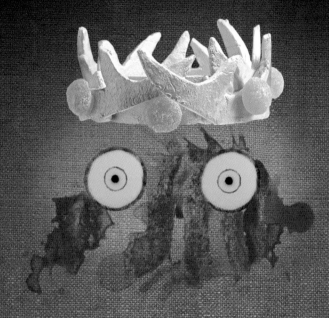

# FOLLOW US

Twitter: @gameofscones_

facebook:

www.facebook.com/GameofScones1

#gameofscones

## Author's Note

This book is a loving tribute from a superfan and not intended to lay claim to the masterful creations of the books or TV programme on which it comments.

I love *Game of Thrones* and I love baking and what better way to pay homage to the show (and make my own unique comment on it) than to bring the two together?

I would like to think that, if only in some miniscule way, the doughy, sugary, (I hope) tasty treats within these pages bring to life the genius of the show in an interesting and enjoyable way.

Bon appetit and remember . . . Dinner is coming!

Jammy Lannister
June 2015

With thanks to...

Anna Valentine
(Hand of the King)

Emma Stark-Smith

Alice Morley
(the King-slayer)

Mark McGinlay

and all the team
at House Orion

Not forgetting...

Maester Trumper

Ser Jammy Lannister is a Knight of Westeros, a long-standing member of the Kingsguard and one of the finest bakers in the Seven Kingdoms.

Having lost his right hand in a tragic accident involving spun sugar, he went on to become the greatest egg beater this side of the Narrow Sea.

He currently lives in King's Landing with his sister.
(They are just really good friends...)

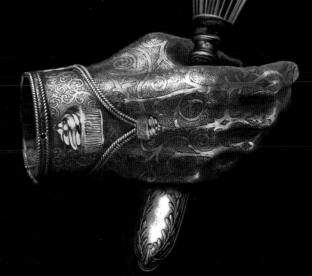

# Enjoyed Game of Scones?
## You'll love this...

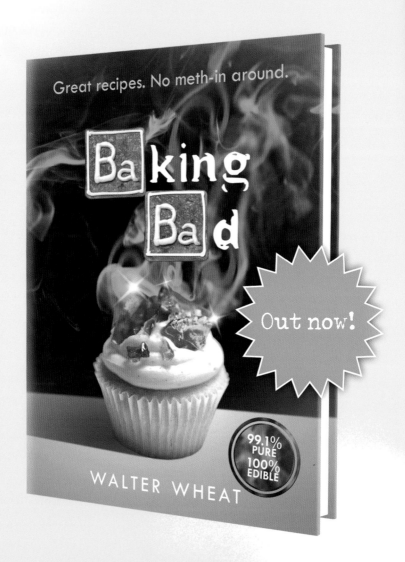